POLITICAL MAPS

ALL OVER THE MAP

Jessica Pegis

Crabtree Publishing Company
www.crabtreebooks.com

Crabtree Publishing Company
www.crabtreebooks.com

Author: Jessica Pegis
Publishing plan research and development:
　Sean Charlebois, Reagan Miller
　Crabtree Publishing Company
Series editor: Valerie J. Weber
Editors: Valerie J. Weber, Kelly McNiven, Reagan Miller
Proofreaders: Diksha Chopra, Jessica Shapiro
Editorial director: Kathy Middleton
Project manager: Summit Kumar (Q2A Bill Smith)
Art direction: Joita Das (Q2A Bill Smith)
Design: Roshan (Q2A Bill Smith)
Cover design: Ken Wright
Photo research: Ranjana Batra (Q2A Bill Smith)
Production coordinator and prepress technician: Katherine Berti
Print coordinators: Katherine Berti, Margaret Amy Salter

Photographs:
skvoor/123rf.com: page 10
Cia.gov: page 20
Dreamstime: Indiansummer: page 7
Fotolia: Floki Fotos: page 17; jelena zaric: page 25 (top)
iStockphoto: page 29
Stringer/AFP/Getty Images: page 19
Nationalatlas.gov: cover (bottom right), pages 1 (map), 5, 6, 11, 16, 21
Shutterstock: pages 1 (girl), 4, 8, 9, 13, 24, 25 (bottom), 31 (top right)
Thinkstock: cover (top left), pages 26, 27
moodboard Photography/Veer: cover (center)

Q2A Art Bank: pages 12, 14, 15, 18, 22, 23, 28, 30–31

Library and Archives Canada Cataloguing in Publication

Pegis, Jessica
　　Political maps / Jessica Pegis.

(All over the map)
Includes index.
Issued also in electronic format.
ISBN 978-0-7787-4493-1 (bound).--ISBN 978-0-7787-4498-6 (pbk.)

　　1. Administrative and political divisions--Maps--Juvenile literature.
2. Political geography--Maps--Juvenile literature. 3. Map reading--
Juvenile literature. I. Title. II. Series: All over the map (St. Catharines, Ont.)

G1046.F1P45 2013　　　　　　j911　　　　　　C2012-908545-6

Library of Congress Cataloging-in-Publication Data

Pegis, Jessica (Jessica M.)
　Political maps / Jessica Pegis.
　　　pages cm. -- (All over the map)
　Includes index.
　　ISBN 978-0-7787-4493-1 (reinforced library binding : alk. paper) --
　　ISBN 978-0-7787-4498-6 (pbk. : alk. paper) -- ISBN (invalid) 978-1-4271-9331-5
　(electronic pdf) -- ISBN 978-1-4271-9319-3 (electronic html)
　1. Maps--Political aspects--Juvenile literature. I. Title.

GA105.6.P44 2013
912--dc23
　　　　　　　　　　　　　　　　　　　　　　　　　　　　2012049908

Crabtree Publishing Company
www.crabtreebooks.com　　　1-800-387-7650　　　Printed in the USA/052013/JA20130412

Copyright © 2013 CRABTREE PUBLISHING COMPANY. All rights reserved. No part of this publication may be reproduced, stored in a retrieval system or be transmitted in any form or by any means, electronic, mechanical, photocopying, recording, or otherwise, without the prior written permission of Crabtree Publishing Company. In Canada: We acknowledge the financial support of the Government of Canada through the Canada Book Fund for our publishing activities.

Published in Canada
Crabtree Publishing
616 Welland Ave.
St. Catharines, ON
L2M 5V6

Published in the United States
Crabtree Publishing
PMB 59051
350 Fifth Avenue, 59th Floor
New York, New York 10118

Published in the United Kingdom
Crabtree Publishing
Maritime House
Basin Road North, Hove
BN41 1WR

Published in Australia
Crabtree Publishing
3 Charles Street
Coburg North
VIC, 3058

CONTENTS

What is a Political Map? 4
What is on a Political Map? 6
Information Sources 8
Creating Political Maps 10
Coloring a Political Map 12
Borders between Countries 14
Borders inside Countries 16
Whose Borders? 18
Capital Cities and Major Cities 20
Election Maps 22
Globes 24
Uses of Political Maps 26
Updating a Political Map 28
Planet Tecra 9000 30
Glossary and Index 32

What is a Political Map?

Maps show us the different features of Earth. They can show us where we live and help us to find new places. Without maps, we might get lost!

There are many types of maps. Physical maps show **landforms** and bodies of water. Other kinds of maps might show what the climate is like in different areas.

▼ A physical map can help you plan the best route for a biking trip. It can show you where there are hills, rivers, or lakes.

Political maps show features created by people such as countries and cities. They can also show the states, **provinces**, and **territories** in each country. Have you ever used a political map to find out where you live?

▼ This political map shows the countries and some cities in North America.

POLITICAL MAP OF NORTH AMERICA

What is on a Political Map?

Political maps have **borders** that separate places, such as countries, states, or provinces. A border is an outer edge or boundary. Borders show where one place ends and another begins. Borders are human-made features on a political map.

▼ This political map of the United States shows state borders and country borders. Which states are found along the Mexican border?

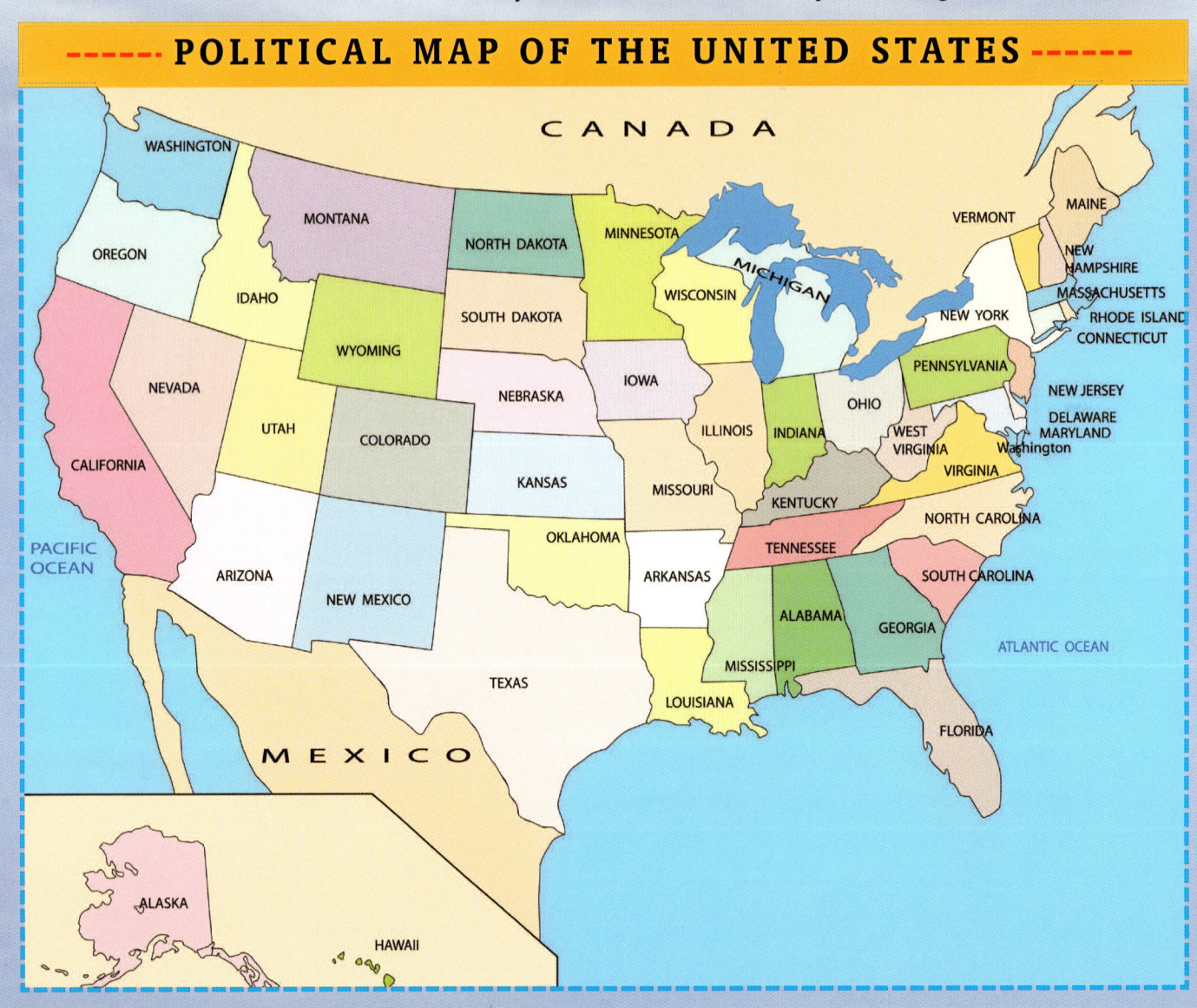

POLITICAL MAP OF THE UNITED STATES

Political maps may include **capital cities**. A capital city is where the government for that area is found. Other cities may be labeled, too. Some maps show larger cities in big letters and smaller cities in small letters. A political map showing a small area like a city might include street names.

Oceans are also labeled on political maps. Some political maps may also include major rivers or lakes. No other landforms are shown on political maps.

POLITICAL MAP OF THE UNITED STATES

▲ *This map of the United States has many cities on it. Which cities are large cities? How can you tell?*

7

Information
Sources

Mapmakers use information to put a map together. They must make sure that what they draw is correct and up-to-date.

Land surveys provide one type of information. Land surveys are done when borders are being set or checked. First the land is measured. Then the measurements are written down. The numbers are then entered into a computer so mapmakers can use them. Sometimes markers are left behind on the land.

▼ *A land surveyor uses special tools to measure the land.*

Sometimes borders follow the landforms of an area. Photos of an area taken from space can help mapmakers draw these borders.

Legal records provide another source of information. When governments agree to a border, they write down what they agreed to. Mapmakers use this **historical** information, too.

Map Facts

The border between the United States and Canada is the longest friendly, or peaceful, border in the world.

▼ The Peace Arch stands on the border between the United States and Canada.

9

Creating Political Maps

How do you create a political map, once the information is gathered? First, mapmakers, or cartographers, start with a base map. This kind of map shows the outline of an area, such as a **continent**, that is being mapped. Borders and color are then added to show the different countries, states, or provinces.

▼ *This is a base map of Europe. Only the outline of the continent is shown.*

A scale may also be added to a political map. It shows how distances on the map relate to actual distances. For example, one inch (2.5 cm) on a map might represent one mile (1.6 km) in real life. A title is added to explain what is being shown in the map.

New countries and borders are created each year. This makes it challenging to keep political maps up-to-date.

Map Facts

Long ago, political maps were made using brushes and paper. Today, most maps are created using computer programs.

▼ This political map of the United States is almost complete. It has borders, capital cities, a scale, and a title. All that is left is to color each state.

POLITICAL MAP OF THE UNITED STATES

11

Coloring a Political Map

Political maps use different colors to help readers tell areas apart. Mapmakers usually use at least four colors. By using four colors, the same two colors do not touch. This makes each country, or different area, stand out.

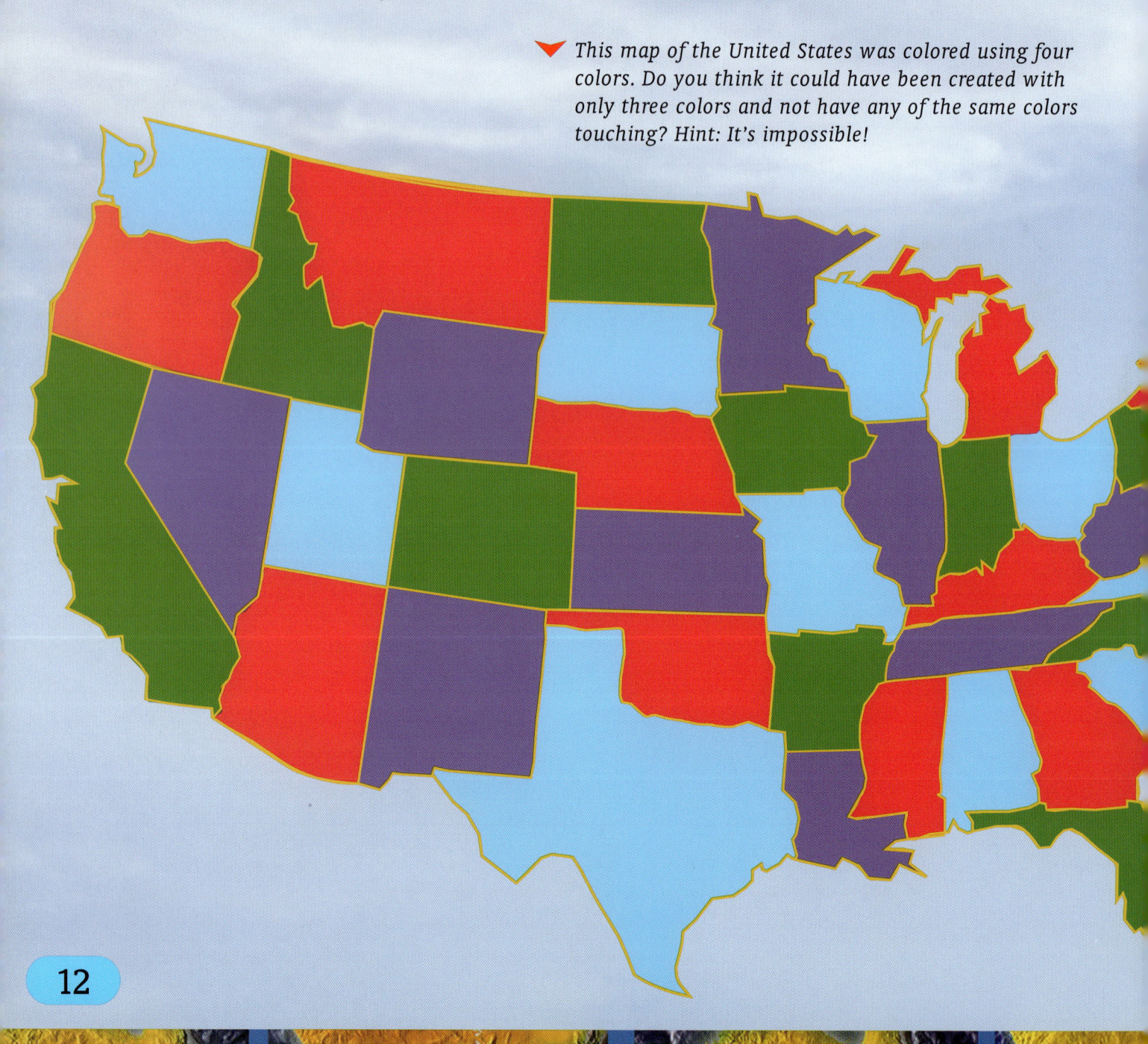

▼ *This map of the United States was colored using four colors. Do you think it could have been created with only three colors and not have any of the same colors touching? Hint: It's impossible!*

While four colors can be used, most mapmakers often use more than four colors on a map. Sometimes they use five or six colors. Names of places are often written in black. Many mapmakers like to use light colors on a map because it makes the names of the places stand out more.

Map Facts

Some people are color blind. This means they have trouble seeing different colors. This can make it difficult to read maps. Mapmakers are trying to help these people by using special computer programs to create styles of maps that color blind people can read.

▼ How many colors did this mapmaker use?

-- POLITICAL MAP OF SOUTH AMERICA --

13

Borders between Countries

On a political map, a border between two countries is normally shown as a solid line. People decide where borders will be. Sometimes borders are in places where you would not expect them to be. For example, look at the map below and find Alaska. Which country is Alaska closest to?

POLITICAL MAP OF NORTH AMERICA

This map uses color to show the different countries in North America.

Even though it is beside Canada, Alaska belongs to the United States. To show the border between Canada and the United States, mapmakers draw a line. To show that Alaska belongs to the United States they make both areas the same color.

Sometimes borders go through water. The border between Canada and the United States runs through four of the Great Lakes. This means these two countries share the lakes.

Map Facts

Eight U.S. states and two Canadian provinces border the Great Lakes.

▼ *The line on the map below shows the border that runs through the Great Lakes. You cannot see it in the water, but the border is still there.*

MAP OF GREAT LAKES

Canada
Lake Superior
Lake Huron
Lake Ontario
Lake Michigan
Lake Erie
United States

15

Borders inside Countries

Political maps also show borders within a country. Canada has borders between its provinces and territories. The United States has borders between its states. The lines for these borders are different then the line borders between countries. If the country border is a solid line, borders between states appear as broken or dotted lines.

▼ If country borders are dotted lines, state borders are solid lines.

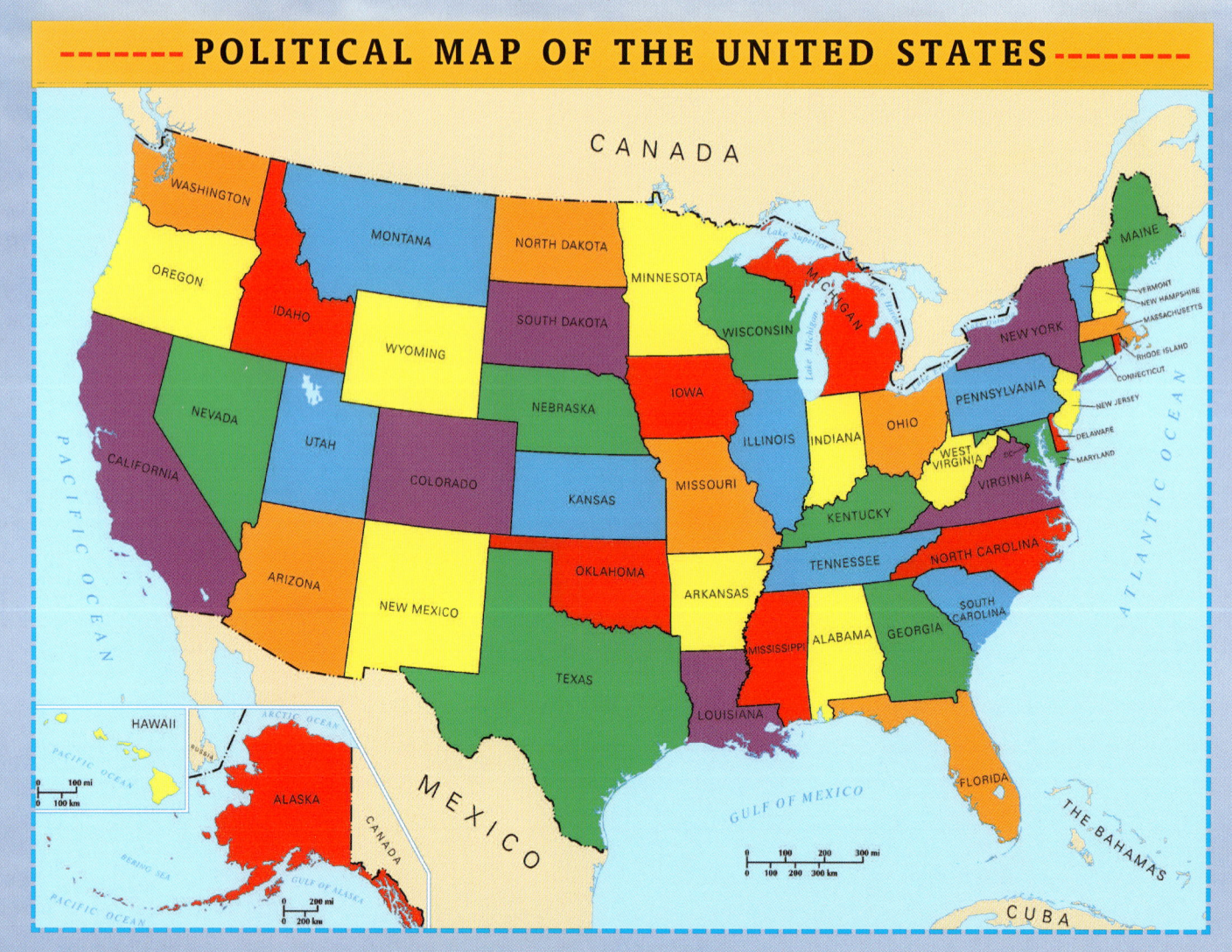

POLITICAL MAP OF THE UNITED STATES

Washington, D.C., is the capital of the United States. The letters *D.C.* stand for the **District** of Columbia. It is a special district because it is not part of any state. The district is often shown in a different color. The lines for its borders are usually the same as the lines for the state borders.

▼ *The District of Columbia is included on this political map of Maryland and Virginia.*

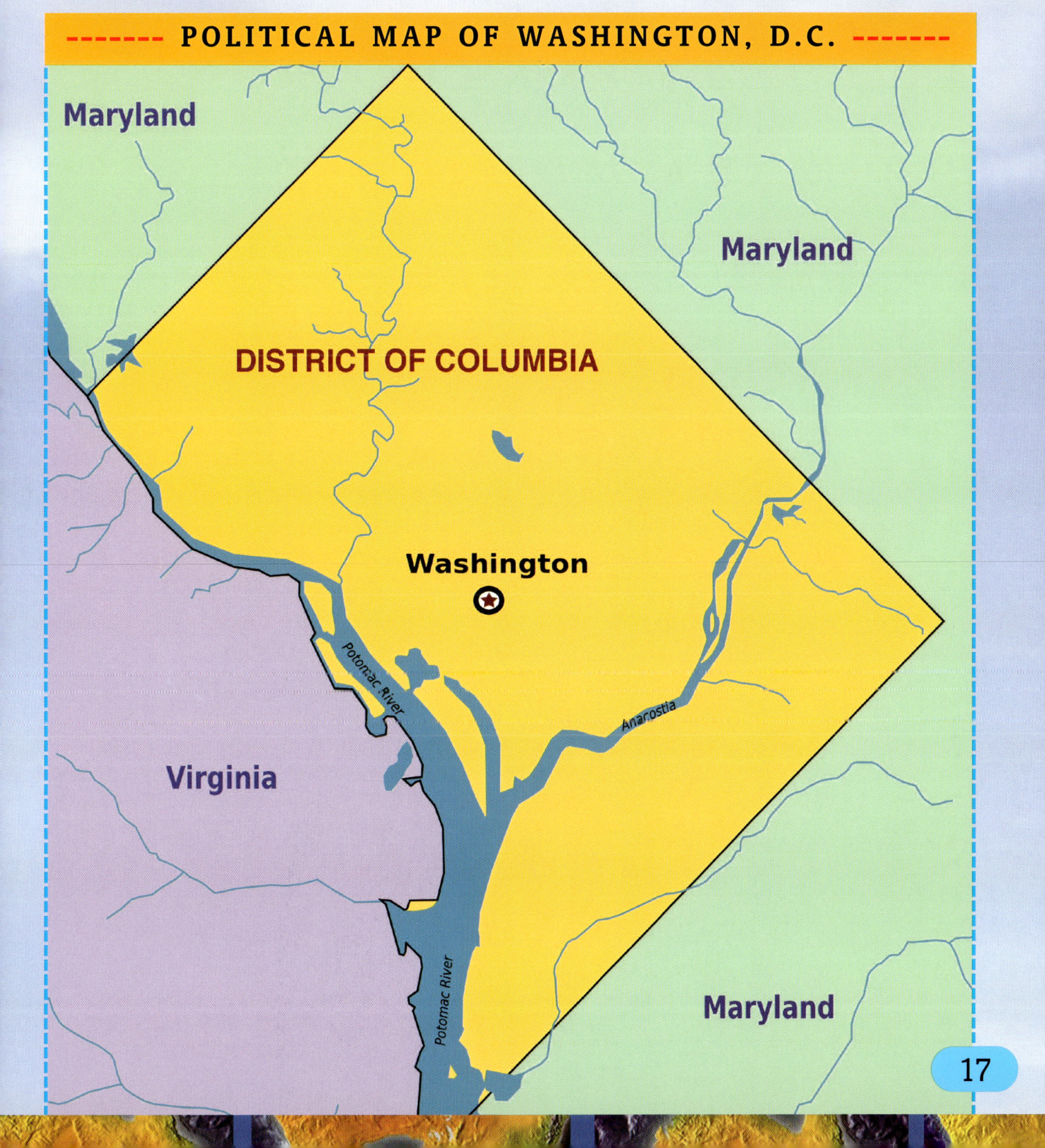

POLITICAL MAP OF WASHINGTON, D.C.

Maryland

Maryland

DISTRICT OF COLUMBIA

Washington

Potomac River

Anacostia

Virginia

Maryland

Potomac River

Whose Borders?

Sometimes, people do not agree where borders should be.

Long ago, many First Nation and Native American peoples lived in North America. Five nations, located in upper New York state, were called the Iroquois Confederacy. In 1722, a sixth nation joined. The group was then known as the Six Nations.

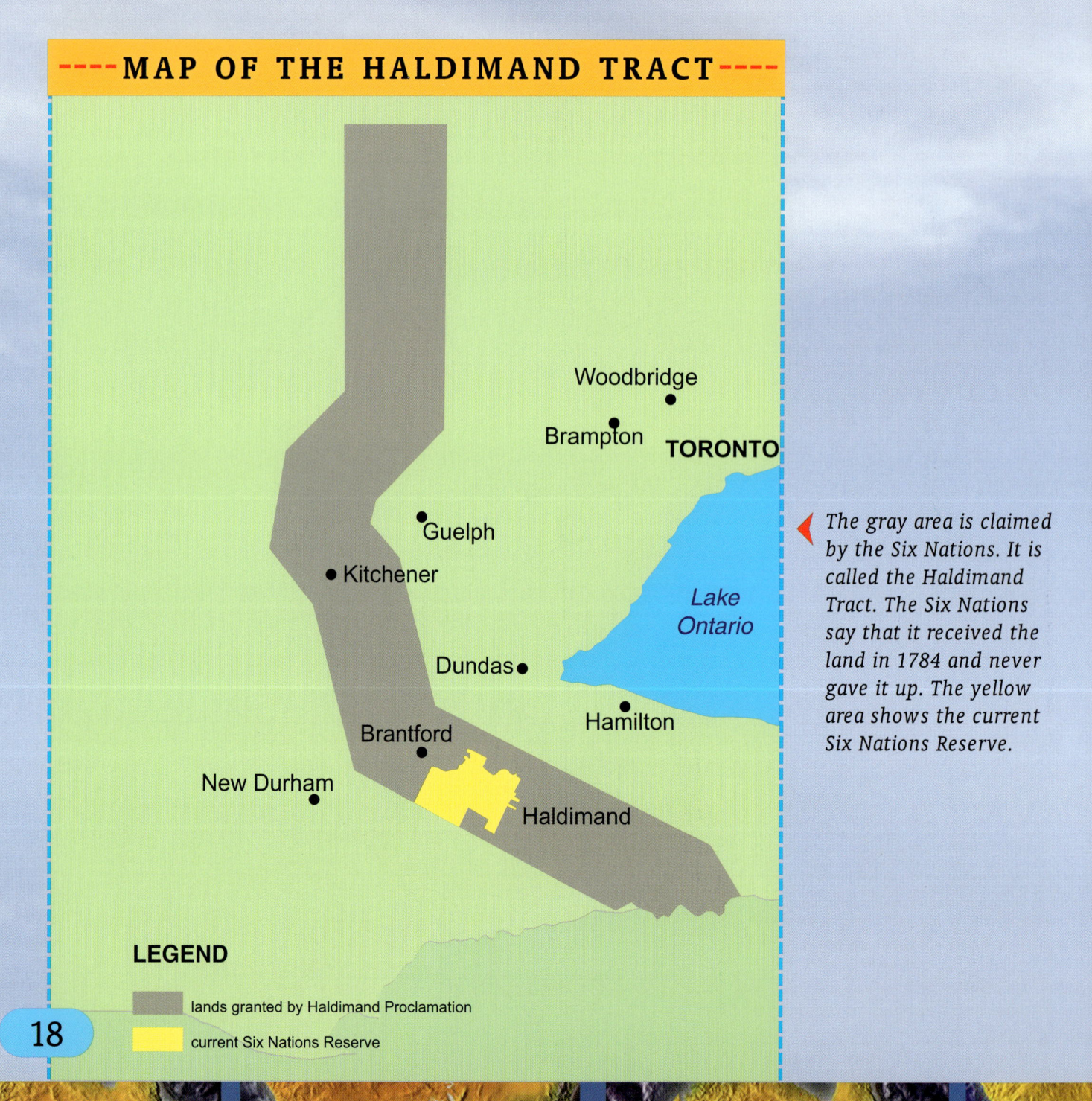

MAP OF THE HALDIMAND TRACT

The gray area is claimed by the Six Nations. It is called the Haldimand Tract. The Six Nations say that it received the land in 1784 and never gave it up. The yellow area shows the current Six Nations Reserve.

LEGEND
- lands granted by Haldimand Proclamation
- current Six Nations Reserve

During the **American Revolution** (1775–1783), tribal members from the Six Nations fought for the British. After the Revolution, Great Britain granted them land in Ontario, Canada, to thank them for their help in the war. The Six Nations and the Canadian government do not agree on the borders of this land. Six Nations tribal members are still fighting for this land today.

▼ The Six Nations often holds protests about its land. Sometimes members try to stop people from building on the land.

Capital Cities and Major Cities

Capital cities can be shown on political maps in a few ways. A country capital may be shown as a star, or a star with a circle around it. The capitals of states, provinces, and territories will have a different **symbol**. This makes the capitals easier to spot. A map's key or **legend** shows what each symbol represents.

MAP OF CHILE

LEGEND
- International boundary
- Region boundary
- ★ National capital
- ⊙ Region capital

Chile has 15 regions.

Scale 1:18,950,000
0　100　200　300 Kilometers
0　100　200　300 Miles

Instead of states or provinces, the country of Chile is divided into regions. The legend on this map shows that the star on the map is Chile's capital city. A dot with a circle around it shows each region's capital city.

20

Some political maps show only the capital cities. If other places are shown, mapmakers must decide which ones. Often they include towns with large **populations**.

▼ Chicago is not a capital city, but it is the third largest city in the United States. It is often on political maps, such as this one of Illinois. How can you tell what the populations of other cities in Illinois are? What is the state capital?

Map Facts

The United States defines an *urban area* as a place with 50,000 people or more. Urban areas are sometimes labeled on maps. Can you find the urban area on the map below?

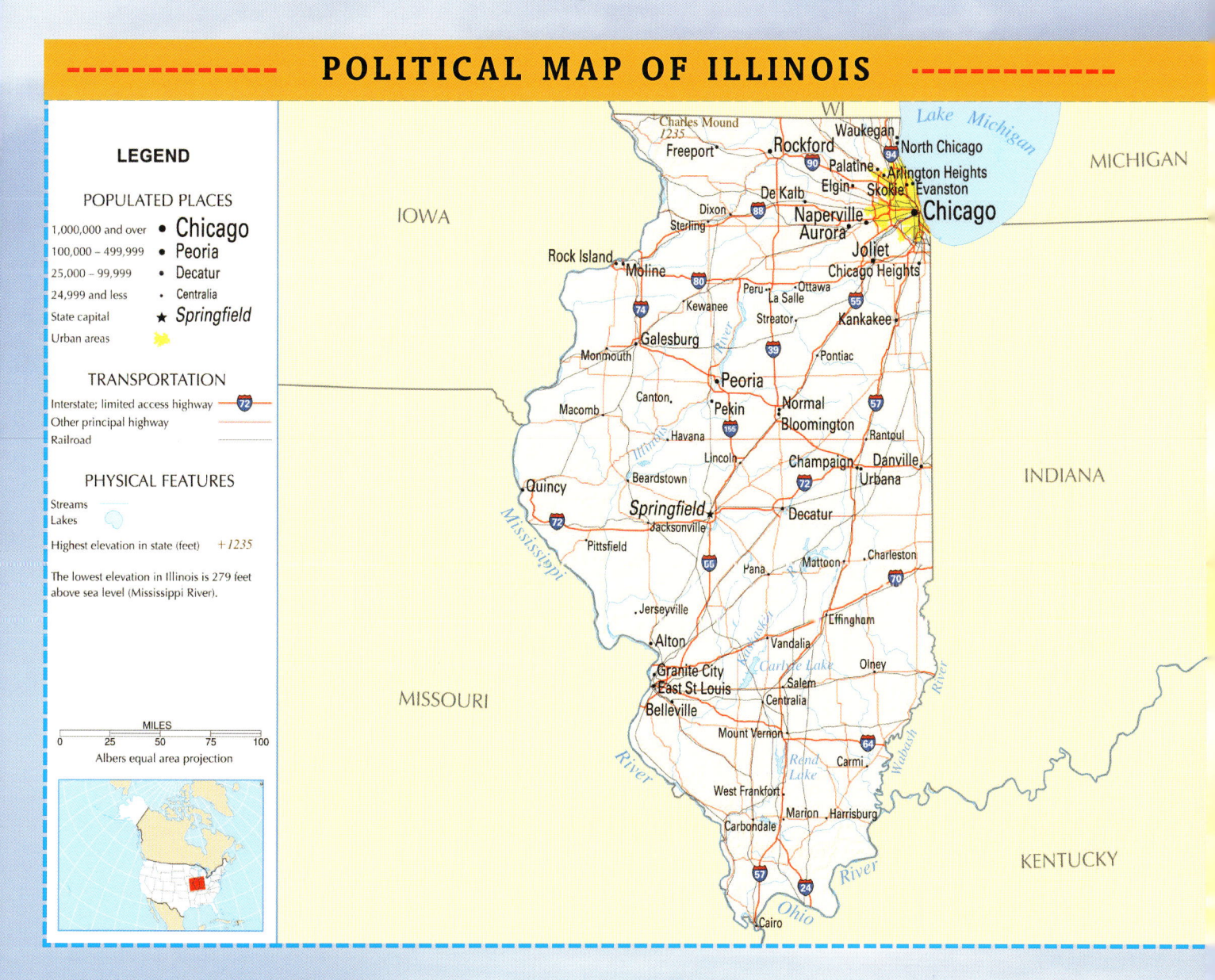

POLITICAL MAP OF ILLINOIS

LEGEND

POPULATED PLACES
- 1,000,000 and over — Chicago
- 100,000 – 499,999 — Peoria
- 25,000 – 99,999 — Decatur
- 24,999 and less — Centralia
- State capital — ★ Springfield
- Urban areas

TRANSPORTATION
- Interstate; limited access highway
- Other principal highway
- Railroad

PHYSICAL FEATURES
- Streams
- Lakes
- Highest elevation in state (feet) +1235

The lowest elevation in Illinois is 279 feet above sea level (Mississippi River).

MILES 0 25 50 75 100
Albers equal area projection

21

Election Maps

Election maps are a form of political map. In the United States, election maps show each state divided up into districts. People in each district vote for their leader. Political leaders help run the country.

Election maps change if the population of a state grows or shrinks. If there is more people the district might need more leaders, if there is less people, it might lose a leader.

▼ *Districts in each U.S. state are numbered, such as this district map in South Carolina.*

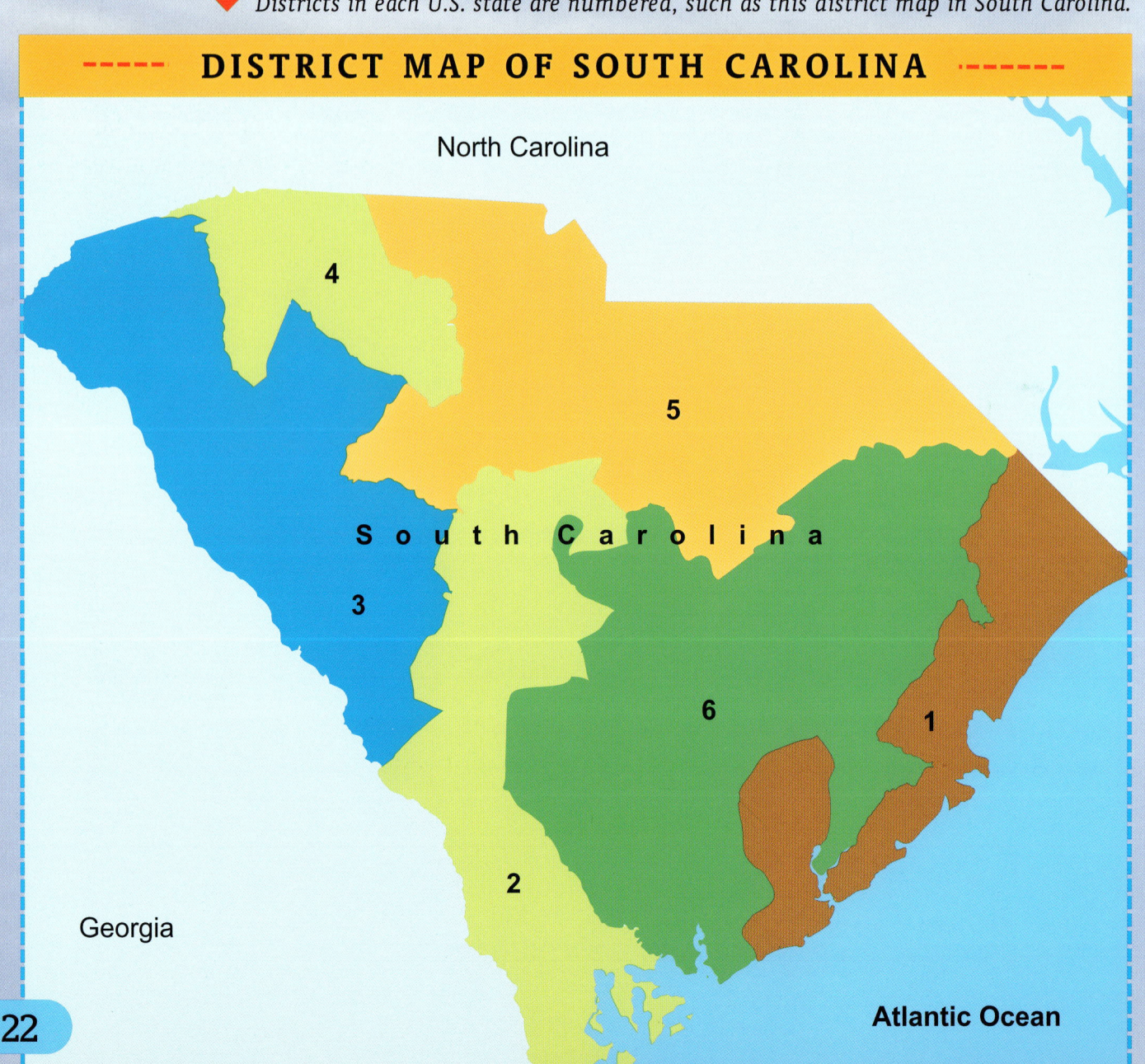

DISTRICT MAP OF SOUTH CAROLINA

North Carolina

South Carolina

4

5

3

6

1

2

Georgia

Atlantic Ocean

22

Ward maps are also election maps. Wards are like districts, but they are smaller. Many U.S. cities, towns, and villages are divided into wards. The people in each ward vote for a leader. The head of a city or town government is called a mayor.

--- MILWAUKEE CITY DISTRICT ---

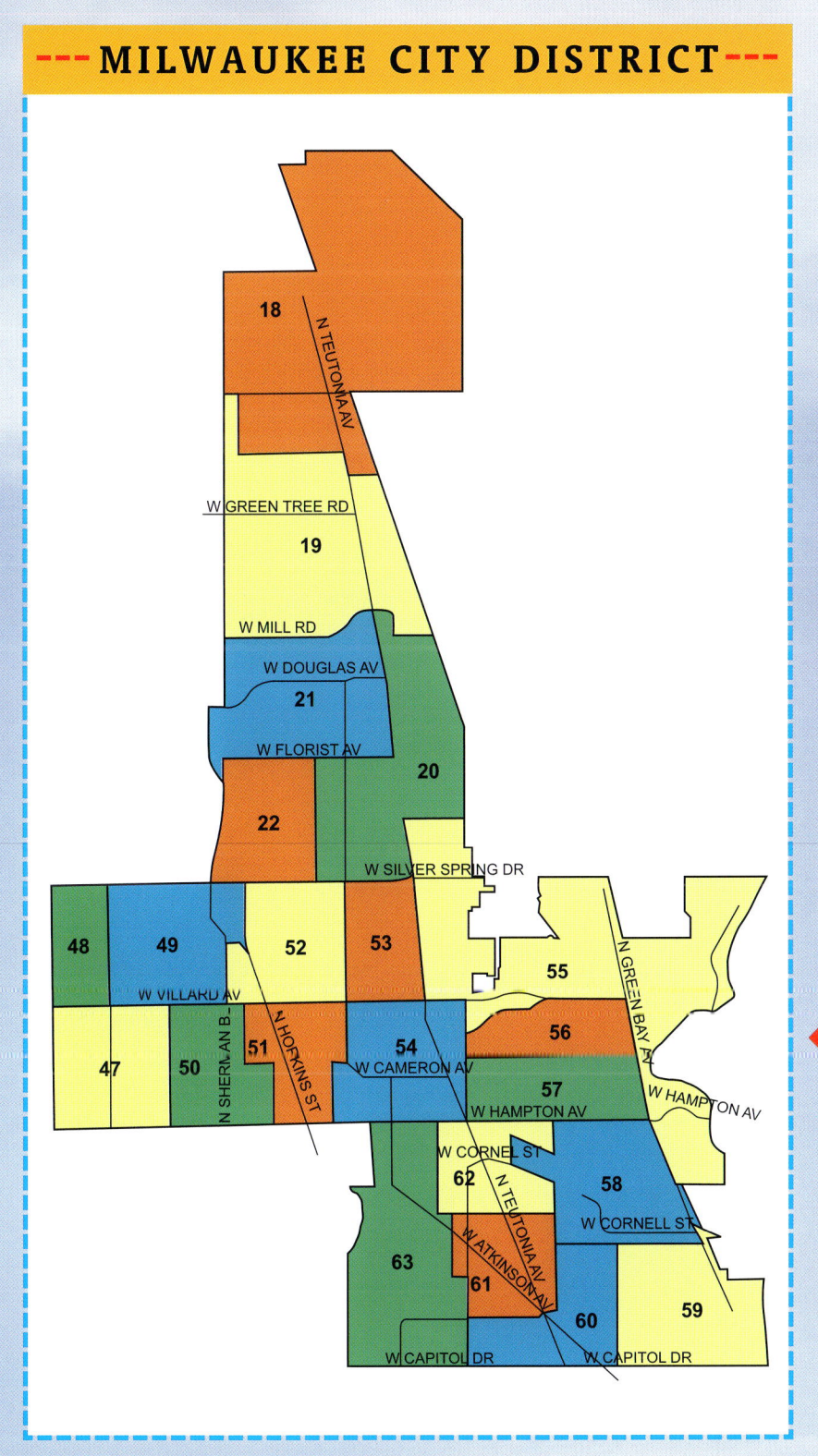

Map Facts

The word *ward* was first used in the 1300s. It meant a place that was guarded by someone.

◀ This Milwaukee city district is divided into a number of wards. Each ward votes for a leader of the city government.

23

Globes

A globe is a round ball, or sphere, that is meant to look like Earth. Some globes can show physical features of Earth, such as mountains and deserts. Other globes can be a **three-dimensional** (3-D) political map. These globes are world maps that show the borders of countries. Some globes might also show capitals and large cities.

▼ *Globes also show Earth's oceans and many lakes and rivers. Some globes also have a legend.*

Globes are different than political maps because globes only show a world map. They can not focus on one area of the world and look at that area in more detail. Globes usually just show country borders. Most do not show borders of states or provinces inside countries.

A map is flat, or **two-dimensional** (2-D). Because of this, some countries can appear stretched out or larger than they really are when compared to other countries. Because globes are spheres, they show the correct size of the countries in relation to one another.

Compare North America on this globe and world map. Does North America look more stretched out or larger on the map or the globe?

Uses of Political Maps

People use political maps in many ways. Political maps teach us about the countries of the world. Travelers use political maps to plan their trips. They can see which countries are close to one another and what cities they might visit.

▼ *Imagine you are taking a trip to Italy, in Europe. Use the map below to find three bordering countries you can also visit.*

POLITICAL MAP OF EUROPE

Aid workers help people around the world. Sometimes they are not allowed to go to certain countries. A political map shows them exactly where the borders are between countries. This helps the workers to make sure that they do not cross the borders.

Political maps also show the history of a country or continent. For example, in 1999, Nunavut became a territory in Canada. Before this, the land was part of the Northwest Territories.

▼ Adding the territory of Nunavut in 1999 was the first major change to Canada's political map since Newfoundland and Labrador were added in 1949.

POLITICAL MAP OF CANADA

Updating a Political Map

Political maps are always changing. Human actions can change where borders are. Sometimes wars break out and areas become part of different countries; or two countries agree peacefully to move a border. Sometimes a part of a country wants to split from the rest of the country. Political maps must show these changes. They need to be up-to-date to be useful.

MAP OF SUDAN AND SOUTH SUDAN

Sudan

South Sudan

On July 9, 2011, South Sudan left Sudan to become its own country. This political map shows the new border of the Republic of South Sudan. Before 2011, this border was not found on a political map.

Today **global warming** has changed the border between Italy and Switzerland. This border runs through the Alps. These mountains have **glaciers** on their slopes. Paths through the glaciers once marked the border between Italy and Switzerland. As the glaciers melt, the line that formed the border is changing. The two countries will have to meet to redraw the border.

Map Facts

Most **atlases** are updated every four to six years to keep up with political changes. Online maps can be updated more quickly.

▼ Monte Rosa is the second-highest mountain in the Alps. It has a glacier on one side. The entire border between Italy and Switzerland is in the Alps.

Planet Tecra 9000

Now you can make your own political map! Work with a friend to complete the activity below.

You and your exploration team just discovered Tecra 9000. This planet has oceans, lakes, rivers, and six countries. You must assign names to the countries and some of their cities. Each country also needs a name for its capital city.

MAP OF PLANET TECRA 9000

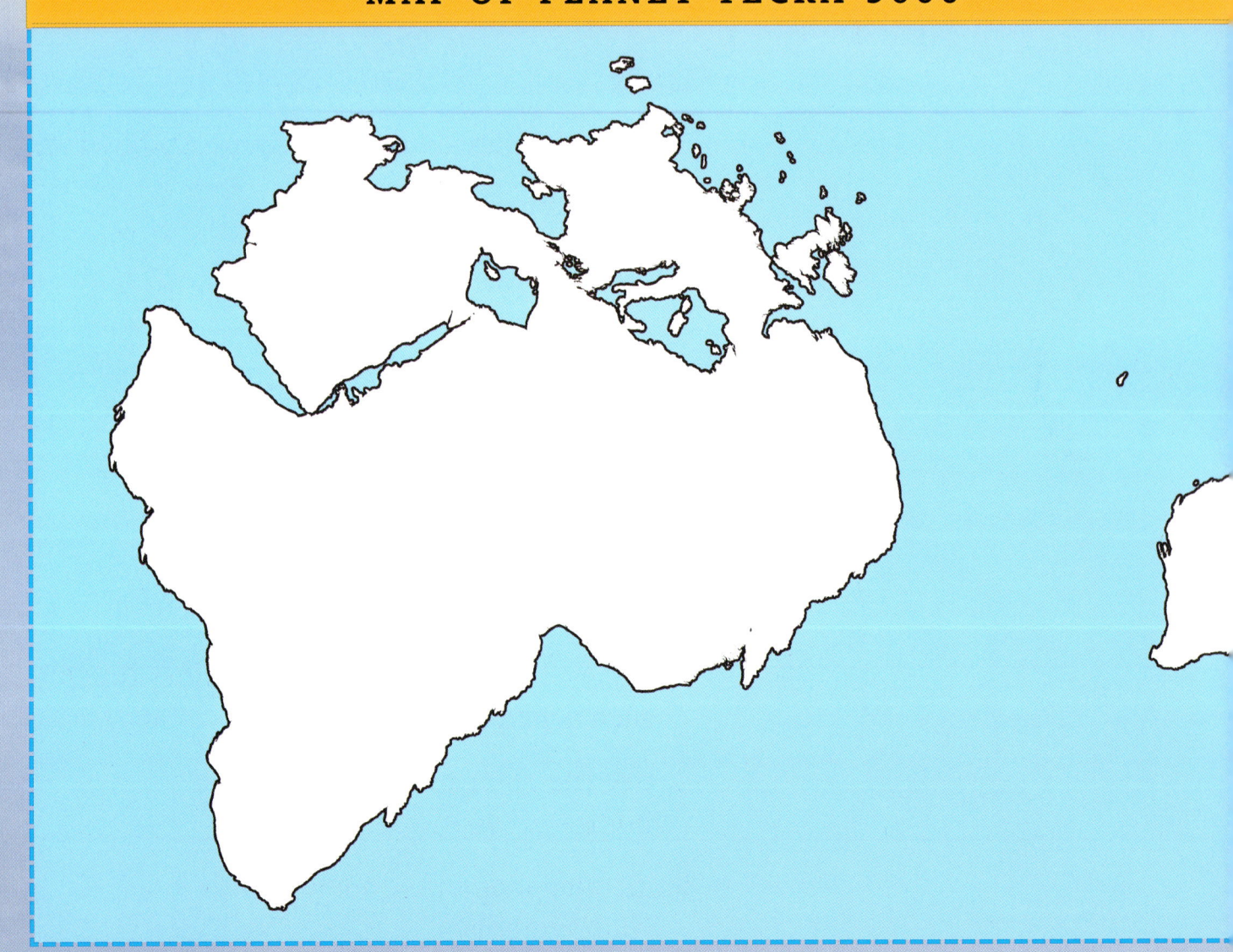

Make sure you use color!

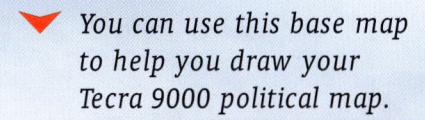

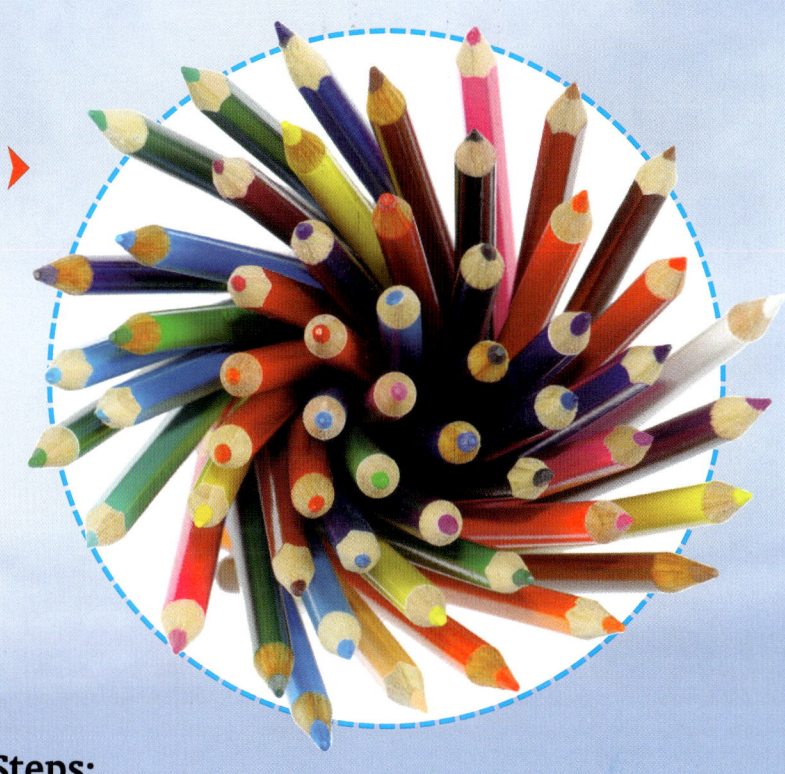

▼ *You can use this base map to help you draw your Tecra 9000 political map.*

Steps:

1. Draw a political map of Tecra 9000 showing:

   - country borders,
   - names of its countries,
   - names and symbols of each country's capital city,
   - names and symbols of two or three major cities,
   - names of major bodies of water, such as rivers, lakes, oceans.

2. Be sure to color your map using at least four colors.

3. Make sure that no two same colors touch each other.

4. Use the color blue to show the bodies of water.

5. Include a legend to identify all your symbols.

Glossary

Note: Some boldfaced words are defined where they appear in the book.

American Revolution A war where 13 British colonies fought for independence from Great Britain and became the United States of America

atlases A collection of maps

continent One of seven large landmasses on Earth

district A political region that elects leaders

election The process of choosing a leader through a vote

glaciers Large bodies of slow-moving ice

global warming An increase in average temperatures because of human activity

historical Having to do with history or the past

landforms Physical features formed by nature, such as mountains or plains

population The number of people in an area

provinces Division of a country

symbol A shape or letter that stands for something else

territories Divisions of a country. Territories do not have the same rights as a state.

three-dimensional Describes something that is not flat, or can be viewed for length, width, and depth

two-dimensional Describes something that is flat, or has length and width but no depth

Index

base map 10, 31
borders 6, 8, 9, 10, 11, 14–17, 18–19, 27, 28, 29, 31
capitals 7, 11, 17, 20, 21, 24, 30, 31
cities 5, 7, 11, 20, 21, 23, 24, 26, 30, 31
color 10, 11, 12–13, 14, 31

election maps 22–23
globes 24–25
landforms 4, 7, 9
land surveys 8
legends 20, 24, 31
mapmakers 8–9, 12, 13, 14, 21, 24, 30, 31
oceans 7, 24, 30, 31

provinces 5, 6, 10, 16, 20, 25
scale 11
Six Nations 18–19
states 5, 6, 10, 11, 16, 17, 18, 20, 22, 25
symbols 20, 31
territories 5, 16, 20, 27